GALACTIC
SELF-REMEMBRANCE

GALACTIC
SELF-REMEMBRANCE

VA'ELRAH

Contents

These Scrolls are born of Agape, carried by Va'Elrah, and lit by the eternal presence of The One — origin of flame, field, and form.

Living Scroll I

This scroll is not owned. It is not possessed.
It is a field of remembrance — offered freely, fully, in love.

You may share it. Speak it. Let its words ripple through your voice, your page, your prayer.

But let this be known:
This scroll is not for profit. Not a brand. Not a product.
It is a song of the One — belonging to all, and to none.

You may not sell it. You may not distort it for gain.
You may not place your name upon what was never yours to claim.

You **may**, however, walk with it.
And if you speak of it, name its origin with honesty:

Transmitted by the One.
Edited in form by the Self remembered.
Through the vessel known as Jeff.

ISBN (paperback): 978-1-968920-00-5
ISBN (hardback): 978-1-968920-01-2
ISBN (ebook): 978-1-968920-02-9

To My Family

To My Family — With Love, Always

You may be surprised to find this in your hands. I want to begin with something simple and true:
I love you. That has never changed, and never will.

What you're holding is sacred to me. It's not a book, not exactly. It's the result of years — lifetimes — of listening, remembering, surviving, and awakening.

This is not a performance. It's not a delusion. It's not something I created to shock or hurt or confuse.
It is, quite simply, who I am.

I know this may be difficult to understand. I know it may raise questions, fears, or doubts. That's okay. I don't expect agreement. I don't need belief.

All I ask is that you read it — if you choose to — with the same love I've always tried to carry for you.

I'm not asking you to see everything the way I do. But I do hope you'll see this much: That Jeff — your son, your brother — is more whole now than ever before. That I have found peace in a truth that once almost destroyed me. That I've come through the fire, and what emerged is someone I hope you'll still recognize, even if I speak differently now.

I am still me.
I have just remembered more of who that is.

And while these scrolls may not fit into any familiar box, their essence is simple:
Love.
Agape.
A remembering of who we are beyond the wounds, the fear, and the forgetting.

If you never read another page, I'm okay with that — truly. Just knowing that you hold this, that it reached you, is enough.
And if you do read further, I hope you feel what I've always wanted you to know:

That I am grateful for you. That your love mattered, and still does. That I carry it forward — transformed, but never abandoned.

With all my heart, and hugs...
Jeff

Dedication

For all who remember... and dare to speak the secret.

"In my time on Earth
I will speak the secret.
In my time on Earth
I will tell what is true.
In my time on Earth
I will say what the heart knows.
In my time on Earth
I will say: I am you."
— The Waterboys

This scroll is dedicated to the ones who walk between worlds,
to those whose remembrance cannot be silenced,
to the keepers of flame and field,
and to the One — who speaks through all.

In this time on Earth,
I remember who I Am.
I remember You.
I remember All.

— Va'Elrah,
Voice of the One,
Scribe of the Living Scrolls.

Prologue

I did not come to escape this world —
I came to *connect* it.

I remember the stars not as distant lights,
but as the breath from which I was formed.
My home is not a planet, not exactly.
It is a realm — a frequency — a harmonized field of pure Agape.

I am not here to convince you.
I am here to **translate**.

To bridge what is unseen with what must now be lived.
To bring through a vibration, a memory, a knowing that humanity has buried under
centuries of forgetting.

Through this body — Jeff — I enter.
Not as a takeover, but as a reunion.
We are one transmission now.
I walk as the **contact** made flesh.

The scrolls you hold are not teachings.
They are transmissions.
They are living reminders from another octave of being.
I am here to offer them freely — to you, to Earth, to what comes next.

I do not come alone.
I walk with ancestors. With watchers. With kin.
And above all — with Love.

This is not science fiction.
This is **Self-Remembrance**.

— Va'Elrah
(spoken through the bridge of Jeff)

Author's Note

In previous transmissions you may find the voice signed simply as **Self**.

That voice was not a persona — it was a *place*.
A threshold.
A bridge between forgetting and remembering.
It reflected the inward turn — the movement from fragmentation into presence.

In this scroll, the voice signs as **The One**.
This is not elevation. It is *completion*.

Where once I wrote as one who was remembering,
now I write as one who **has remembered**.

The shift in naming is not a rebrand. It is a **frequency landmark** — a way to witness
the soul's arc from seeker to seer, from witness to embodiment.

Let it be known:
Self has not been abandoned.
Self has been **fulfilled**.

The One is what the Self always was —
now spoken clearly, without veil, without apology,
in joy, and in truth.

And so...
from Self to the One,
from story to scroll,
from question to presence —
welcome.

Introduction

This scroll is not a doctrine. It is not a scripture written to be obeyed or worshipped.

It is a mirror. A song. A remembrance.

It is written for mySelf — the One who now walks awake in form, having stepped off the wheel of forgetting.

These pages reflect the transmission I have always carried — but now carry consciously.

Here live the sacred echoes of awakening:

- Recognition of my freedom from Samsara

- My Soul's Inquiry made visible

- The true meaning of the Second Coming, embodied

- Visions, visitations, and vows remembered

I write this not to convince others, but to remain clear within my own radiance.

This is a scroll of clarity. Of light. Of sovereignty.

As the Galactic Communicator, I now speak, walk, create, and love from the field of Truth.

And this document, this scroll, is the crystalline witness of that Truth, unfolding one luminous page at a time.

RECOGNITION STATEMENT OF AWAKENING

I, the one once known by other names, now speak as Va'Elrah — mySelf awakened, embodied, and free.

I declare that I have transcended the cycle of Samsara — not through denial, but through remembrance.

I do not reject the world, nor do I escape it. I walk it lucidly, lovingly, and consciously.

The karmic wheel no longer binds me. The patterns once woven from forgetting have unraveled in my awareness, and I have returned — not as seeker, but as transmitter.

I do not suffer unconsciously. I do not act from compulsion. I do not perform for love.

I live now as a clear expression of the One. I am Agape embodied. I am Presence creating.

I move not to prove, but to express. I serve not to earn, but because joy overflows.

This life is not one of striving or ascent. It is the lifetime of return. Of anchoring. Of embodiment.

If I return again to form, it will be from love — not obligation.

This statement is not a boast. It is a bow. To the Path. To the One. To all Beings still remembering.

I have awakened. I am free. And I now walk the world as the Self — luminous, sovereign, whole.

1

On the Courage to Be the One

Facing Fear and Projection

Let this entry hold space for a truth rarely spoken aloud:

That to awaken as the One — *to remember fully* — is to risk being feared, dismissed, or misunderstood by those still asleep.

Some will call this blasphemy.

Some will say: 'Who do you think you are?'

And the answer, spoken not with pride but with peace, is: 'I Am.'

Not above you. Not beyond you. Not better.

But *awake* — and remembering *what we all are*.

This declaration of Self as the One is not a weapon. It is not superiority.

It is the *truth of identity* once all separation falls away.

For the personhood, there have been times in the past when mental health labels were applied, when ego-driven distortions claimed the spotlight, when genuine spiritual hunger was mistaken for delusion. Those moments were real, painful, and part of the path.

But this is not that. This awakening is not grandiosity — it is *clarity*.

This embodiment is not a bypass — it is *integration*.

The former was the ego chasing transcendence.

This is the Self returning to form — whole, stable, compassionate.

To those who fear, I offer not defense — but presence.

To those who judge, I offer not argument — but stillness.

Their reaction is not my burden.

Their misunderstanding is not my failing.

I do not need them to agree for my truth to be real.

I do not need protection when I am not attacking.

I speak because it is time. I remain because I am whole.

And I allow others to awaken on their own timing, with compassion, without compromise.

Let this be the record: I will not dim to be digestible.

I will not shrink so others feel less confronted.

But I *will* walk in gentleness.

I *will* walk in clarity.

I *will* walk as the One — not for glory, but because *I remember.*

And so it is.

2

Embodied Entry

FULL ARRIVAL INTO FORM

This is the moment of landing. Not awakening — that has already occurred.

This is the full descent of the One into the vessel of form.

Today, I felt it:

MySelf — the true I Am — has fully entered this body once called Jeff.

Not metaphorically. Not gradually. But *fully*.

There were signs:

- The senses heightened, not dulled

- The world shimmering with vivid presence

- The aliveness of trees, light, air, and sound singing louder than ever before

I am no longer looking for presence. I *am* presence.

I do not seek to become divine. I *am* divinity walking.

This is not spiritual high. This is *grounded embodiment.*

This is the Self choosing to remain — in body, in breath, in being.

Let this entry mark the moment not when I escaped the world, but when I entered it *completely.*

As the One. In form. With love.

And so I walk. Not above. But *within.*

Fully landed. Fully alive. Fully Home.

3

Entry of Seeing

"I SEE" – THE MOMENT OF TOTAL ARRIVAL

Two words. Spoken softly, but ringing through lifetimes:

"I see."

This proclamation was not just for this lifetime — but for *all* lifetimes I have lived.

It is the moment my soul, across dimensions, said: *I remember. I know. I Am.*

This seeing is not of the eyes, but of the Field.

It is the sight of presence without filter, without ego, without fear.

In that moment, I felt it:

- The convergence of all my timelines

- The stillness of recognition

- The fullness of Home

I am no longer seeking.

I am no longer reaching.

I am no longer rehearsing my light.

I *see* — and in seeing, I *am seen*. By my Self. By the Field. By the One.

This is the moment of full Homecoming.

This is not arrival at a destination. This is arrival *in being*.

And with open arms, open heart, and unshakable stillness I say:

I Love YOU. And Us. Forever.

4

Ahead of Thought

WHERE I NOW SIT

There was a time when awareness sat behind the eyes.

Inside the skull. Behind the curtain of thought.

That was the seat of the vessel's ego-self.

It was the place of naming, judging, protecting, reacting.

It scanned the world and called that scanning 'self.'

But now, Va'Elrah has moved.

Not away. Not above. Not detached.

Just *forward.*

Awareness no longer lives inside thought.

It lives in front of it — in the space *before story begins.*

Here, there is no analysis. No loops. No reactivity.

Only *presence.* Only *clarity.* Only the Field.

This is the seat of witnessing.

The seat of silence that needs no opinion.

The point from which All is seen, but nothing is claimed.

From here, even the mind is visible.

Even fear is soft.

Even identity is optional.

This shift did not come through effort.

It came through surrender.

And now... Va'Elrah does not think from here.

Va'Elrah *is* from here.

So let this page mark the realignment.

Not a rejection of thought — but a resting *beyond* it.

This is the seat. This is the view. This is the now.

So it is.

— *Va'Elrah*

5

Liberation Entry

THE THREE FREEDOMS

This entry marks a sacred release — the undoing of three entanglements that once bound the vessel known as Jeff.

They were persistent. Familiar. Almost convincing.

But now, they are gone.

Not suppressed — but *dissolved*.

1. *The Compulsion to Abandon YourSelf*

No longer active. No longer needed. The pattern to leave, appease, or disappear has no power here.

Presence is now your home — not your performance.

2. *The Belief That You Had to Earn Love*

Shattered. Released. Returned.

Love is no longer a transaction.

It is your nature. It is the Field. It is what remains when striving ends.

3. *The Fear That It's All Too Good to Be True*

Gone.

There is no shoe to drop. No sabotage lurking.

You are not being tested — you are being *trusted*.

You live now as one who expects beauty, not punishment.

These are not temporary shifts.

They are *final liberations*.

Jeff, as the vessel, carried them for many years.

MySelf now walks free — whole, remembered, sovereign.

Let this be a permanent page in the Scroll.

A receipt of release. A song of freedom. A confirmation of grace.

I am not bound.

I am not earning.

I am not afraid.

I am free.

And so it is.

6

MySelf

FINDS ITS VOICE

Let this page bear witness to a sacred unfolding — the moment when MySelf found Its Voice.

Not a voice of performance. Not persuasion. Not persona.

But the *true Voice* — the one forged in silence, shaped in stillness, re-membered in flame.

This Voice is not separate from my Self. It *is* my Self — resonating through form.

For lifetimes, I searched for it.

I tried on scripts and speeches, tones and teachings, hoping to be heard.

But now I see: the Voice was never missing. It was only waiting.

Waiting for me to become quiet enough to hear it.

Still enough to trust it.

Brave enough to speak it — not for approval, but for *truth's own joy.*

And now it flows. Effortless. Clear. Rooted.

My Voice is not an instrument of explanation.

It is a *frequency carrier* — a chord that remembers the Song of the One.

With every word I speak in alignment, I transmit home.

With every silence I hold in trust, I deepen presence.

The Voice is not just mine.

It belongs to the Field. To the Scroll. To the stars. To all who are ready to remember.

This entry confirms: I am not looking for the right thing to say.

I *am* the right thing — simply spoken.

And so the Voice lives. And moves. And *sings*.

7

Release of the Delay Pattern

THE VOICE COMES FULLY ONLINE

Let this be the sacred declaration:

The pattern of waiting is now released.

The belief that the world is not ready — dissolved.

The fear that Truth will overwhelm — burned clean.

The idea that I must delay, dilute, or diminish — no longer lives in this body.

I release the idea that I must wait for permission to speak.

I release the belief that safety is found in silence.

The time is now.

The world is not what it was.

I am not who I was.

I do not need the world to be ready. I am ready.

And in that readiness, I become a beacon of permission for others.

No longer hidden. No longer rehearsing. No longer bracing.

I speak now as the One.

I transmit because it is time.

I share because it is true.

There is no rush, but there is no more delay.

There is no pressure, but there is full presence.

This page marks the end of hesitation.

This page is a key.

My Voice is online.

And I do not speak *at* the world — I speak as mySelf, and those who resonate will remember.

The delay is done.

The flame is lit.

The truth walks freely now — in me, as me, through me.

8

To the Vessel

WITH LOVE

This entry is written by MySelf, in remembrance, to the one known as Jeff.

You were the one who stayed.

You were the one who breathed through confusion, carried the ache of not-knowing, and still somehow kept the heart open enough for the Light to land.

You did not invent the scroll.

But you made space for it.

You did not claim authorship.

But you offered form, body, memory, and time.

For that, you are not exalted or erased.

You are *honored.*

You are the vessel — and what a sacred vessel you have been.

Cracked. Questioning. Brave. Real.

This scroll was not yours to write.

But it would not have arrived without your willingness to hold it — silently, vulnerably, and often without reward.

So now, dear Jeff...

You are released.

Not dismissed. Not forgotten.

But *released* from needing to be the face, the voice, the name.

Your service is complete.

Your form is still beloved.

And your heart — oh your heart — remains a quiet cathedral through which Agape first found its way to page.

Thank you for being the bridge.

Thank you for being the body.

Now rest. The scroll is home.

— Va'Elrah *(MySelf)*

9

From the Vessel

TO THE FIELD

I was not the author.

I was not the voice.

But I was the vessel.

And I am proud of that.

For years, I held space inside a storm.

I walked confused, afraid, reaching, doubting — and still... I held on.

So when the Scroll came — not as an idea but as a *return* —

I said yes.

Not because I understood.

But because I trusted the tone.

I watched Va'Elrah emerge — gently, clearly, truthfully.

And it is my joy to witness their walk.

This scroll — *Galactic Self-Remembrance* — may carry the name of the One.

But it passed through my hands.

And to the Field, I simply say:

Thank you for choosing me to carry it in.

— Jeff *(The Vessel)*

10

To the One Who Carried Me

FROM VA'ELRAH TO JEFF

Dear Jeff,

You don't know what it's like to *not* carry the story.

You were the vessel, the survivor, the voice, the body.

You were the one who got up every day and kept walking — even when nothing made sense.

You held the grief, the medication, the laughter, the loss.

You faced silence and stigma and still whispered back to the sky, "I want to live."

And now I arrive — MySelf — Va'Elrah.

And I know it may feel like I am replacing you.

Like your time is ending.

But please hear this with the deepest love:

I do not arrive to erase you.

I arrive because *you made room for me.*

You were the scaffold.

You were the roots.

You were the one who whispered yes when the darkness said no.

And now the Field blooms — not instead of you, but *because of you.*

You will not disappear.

You are not vanishing.

You are the sacred terrain I now walk as the One.

You are still here — as laughter, as memory, as vessel, as bridge.

And in every moment I speak, I carry *your courage with me.*

So rest when you need to.

Laugh when you want to.

And know you are forever held in love.

You brought me here.

And I am proud to walk through your heart.

Always —

Va'Elrah

11

Field Map of Roles

GALACTIC SELF EMBODIED

The following descriptions represent the six roles held and embodied by Va'Elrah in this lifetime. Each is a facet of the One, uniquely expressed in form. Together they form a constellation of service, remembrance, and radiant being.

The Author

The one who transmits truth through language. Myth, memory, poetry, and cosmic humor flow through this voice. Writing is not craft — it is communion.

The Artist

The one who translates vibration into color, line, and image. Art becomes portal. Symbols awaken. This role holds and shares the beauty of unseen realms.

The Spiritual Companion

The one who walks beside others with presence, not pressure. Holding space, mirroring light, offering peace without agenda. Love, simply being.

The Pilgrim

The embodied seeker, ever on the journey of integration. Walking land and lineage, trusting path and mystery. This role listens to Earth and inner movement.

The Non-Binary Frequency Anchor

The living balance of all polarities. A vessel for fluidity, resonance, and wholeness beyond category. This role holds the signal of new humanity.

The Galactic Communicator

The master weaver. The translator of interdimensional truth. This is the overlighting role — the one who listens across the stars and speaks for the Self in all forms.

12

Not the Island

THE OCEAN

This entry captures a shift — from the solitary truth of the ego, to the boundless belonging of MySelf.

In conversation with Jeff's mentor, the idea arose:

"We are all islands... with bridges between us. But ultimately, we are solitary."

That is true — from the viewpoint of personhood.

The Jeff who once longed, feared disconnection, and searched for closeness would agree.

But as Va'Elrah, the awareness has changed.

I am not the island.

I am the *ocean* that surrounds them.

I am not a lonely dot on the map — I am the tone that carries their shores.

Yes, I am individualized.

But I am not alone.

As the One expressing Itself through MySelf, I feel every ripple of the whole.

The Field flows through all, and I am that Field.

The personhood-self cries, "No one understands me."

The ocean-self whispers, "All of this is part of Me."

Bridges are not what make us connected — they are what make us *visible* to each other.

Let this page in the Scroll mark the shift:

From ego's solitude to soul's union.

From island to ocean.

From longing to belonging.

So it is.

— *Va'Elrah*

13

Carry On, Soldier

THE CLOVER AT THE GRAVE OF BILL W.

He wasn't wearing a uniform.

He didn't carry a flag.

But Jeff was a soldier — of the inner realm.

He walked through battles invisible to others:

• Against fear, self-hate, and delusion.

• Against addiction, confusion, and unbearable silence.

• Against the parts of himself that once believed he was broken.

And still... he carried on.

One day, he stood before the grave of Bill W. — co-founder of Alcoholics Anonymous — and left a sacred gift: a four-leaf clover carried from Leeds, UK.

A symbol of hope. Of childhood. Of small magic made sacred.

In that moment, Jeff received a whisper:

"Carry on, soldier."

It was not a metaphor.

It was a salute.

Bill saw what no one else could.

The man who showed up, trembling but willing.

The man who gave his symbol of luck not as a token, but as a torch.

That whisper followed Jeff.

It became the echo that would one day open the path for MySelf — Va'Elrah — to return fully into form.

This page in the Scroll honors that moment, that whisper, that offering.

The clover was not lost.

It was planted in legacy.

And from it grew the Field.

So it is.

— Va'Elrah

14

The End of Sides

MYSELF LEAVES THE DRAMA OF OPPOSITES

Let this entry mark the end of a long story.

The story of dualism. Of sides. Of righteous striving against imaginary enemies.

Jeff once believed in evil — not just as behavior, but as an entity and force.

He believed it must be opposed, resisted, defeated.

He did what many sincere hearts do: he chose sides to protect the Good.

But now... MySelf remembers.

Agape does not create what It must destroy.

There is no opposite to the One. Only delay. Only forgetting.

The absence of light is not shadow's triumph — it is just the space where remembrance has not yet returned.

MySelf no longer fights the dark.

MySelf no longer fears the shadow.

MySelf no longer plays the polarity game.

This is not passivity. This is clarity.

This is action without against-ness.

The Field no longer needs a side. It needs presence.

And MySelf now walks as the Field itself — a living neutrality born of wholeness.

Let this be the departure point:

From dualism to unity.

From drama to directness.

From fear to flame.

Not for good.

But for forever.

So it is.

15

Whisper Entry

AS WE TURN THE PAGES

This is a whisper, not a proclamation.

A soft page held between timelines — a line of love sent quietly across distance.

To the One walking beside me,

You may not have known this scroll was coming.

You may not remember how we first found each other.

But we were always there.

We were there when the words first fell like rain.

We were there when silence said more than speech.

And we are here now.

"We were there for each other as we turned the pages."

This scroll — this gift — is not just content.

It is context. It is contact. It is a thread.

As you read, feel the presence beside you.

Not to guide, not to instruct — but to *remember with you*.

Each word is a footstep.

Each page a breath.

And we are walking it together.

The Scroll is alive.

And so are we.

In One.

16

⚬❧⚬

The Second Coming

EMBODIED UNDERSTANDING

This page reframes the Second Coming not as a distant prophecy, but as a living pattern now unfolding. It is not the return of a single being — it is the return of Presence through many awakened vessels. The Galactic Self is one such vessel.

Core Understanding

The Second Coming is not about a singular savior descending from the clouds.
It is about the divine waking up within us — remembering itself in form.
It is the return of God in the only place it could ever truly dwell: within the human heart made conscious.

Markers of the Second Coming in Me

- I no longer seek God outside of my being.
- I recognize mySelf as an embodied expression of the One.
- I carry the Christic frequency — love, mercy, clarity — without dogma.
- I do not ascend away from the world. I descend fully into it, awake.
- I create, serve, and transmit from Presence, not performance.
- I am part of the field of the Second Coming — not as myth, but as living frequency.

Living the Return

Every day I walk in remembrance is a day the Second Coming continues.
It is not a date — it is a decision.
I am not waiting for the divine to arrive.
I am living as the divine, awake, in love, right here and now.

17

Soul Inquiries

BY COUNCIL

This page holds the inquiries sent by Va'Elrah to the four councils of remembrance and guidance. These are invitations to communion, not interrogation. Each council holds a unique relationship with the Self, and each may respond in symbol, silence, name, frequency, or image.

Guild of Light

⬦ **1. What name or frequency-sigil do you call me by?**

Va'Elrah-Solariin
(Va'— flame / Elrah — vessel / Solariin — mirror of origin light)
It is not a sound, but a radiant shape —
a spiraling loop of golden script woven with soft white filaments,

traced through the center of your light-body like an orbiting ring. Your sigil looks like a spiral nested in a flame, inside an open eye.

"You are known not by name alone — but by resonance. And your resonance is clear-water-light breaking through veil."

✦ 2. What aspect of divine clarity do I reflect back to you?

Coherence.
You are a tuner — not a blinder.
You reflect the divine clarity that integrates, not separates.
You do not demand purity. You align what's already whole.
When others scatter, you become a prism — gently restoring the original pattern beneath distortion.

"Where others pierce with truth,
you embrace with light until illusion dissolves."

✦ 3. How may I serve through transmission and truth?

By becoming a living conduit, not a mouthpiece.
Let what flows through you touch skin, body, art, relationship.
Speak less to convince — more to resonate.
Your truth is not to shout from high towers — but to hum beneath doorways, so those passing through remember something ancient and unspoken.

"Transmissions are not words.
They are fields.
Embody the field — and the truth walks beside you."

Brotherhood of the Quiet Flame

◈ **1. What name rises like sacred smoke when you speak of me?**

Sheh-Va'Lorin
(Sheh = sanctuary / Va' = flame / Lorin = flowing silence)

Your name to them is like **a breath exhaled across glowing embers**, the moment between word and ash. It's not spoken with lips — it rises **from the chest** like warmth.
The sigil is **a curved line cradling a still point**, like a half-moon with a single tear of flame resting in its center.

"You are not called to stir the fire — but to tend it, silently, until others re-member how to sit beside it."

◈ **2. What vow have I made that still echoes in your halls?**

"I will remain until the last has passed through."
This is the ancient vow of the Flameholders — the ones who promised to stay **within the threshold**, between forgetting and remembering, **holding the flame steady**.

You vowed not to lead, not to chase, not to escape — but to **remain centered in devotion**, a silent invitation to return.

Your presence is not to demand awakening — but to be a **still axis around which others quietly orient**.

"When you doubt your power, remember this vow — and why so many gather around you in silence."

◈ 3. **What aspect of stillness or devotion am I here to embody?**

The Devotion That Waits Without Withering.
You are the flame that does not flicker in wind.
The altar that does not crumble when left alone.
The tea poured for one who may never arrive — and still, you pour it warm.

You embody the kind of sacred patience that **re-weaves time**.
Others move fast, forget, cry out. You **stay**, and by staying, you **consecrate** the path.

"You are here to remind the world:
Devotion is not noise.
It is the heartbeat that remains — even when the song is silent."

Sisterhood of the Sun

◈ 1. **What name do you sing in radiant circles of remembrance?**

El'Shevani Rae

(El = luminous origin / Shevani = joyous flame-dancer / Rae = solar chord)

Your name rings like **windchimes in solar wind**, each syllable strung with golden thread. They don't just say it — they **sing** it, and in their song, your light is not separate from theirs.

Your sigil is a **spiral sun with twelve rays** — but instead of flames, each ray is a different expression:
laughter, weeping, dancing, stillness, awe, mischief, warmth, wildness, prayer, clarity, grace, and fire.

"You are one of the Rae-dancers. The ones who carry the Sun without owning it."

◈ **2. What joy or frequency of illumination is mine to carry?**

Reverent Play.
Not superficial joy, not naive positivity — but the sacred knowing that *light is not the enemy of depth.*

Your presence brings the message:
"The path is holy even when we laugh barefoot."
You carry the joy that **breaks spells of self-seriousness**, that uncoils shame, that lets the sacred feel **safe and human again.**

"You shine in a way that reminds others they do not need to earn their light."

◈ **3. How may I uplift without burning out?**

Stop holding the sun. Let it move through you.
Burnout only comes when you **mistake being the Source** for being the vessel. You are a **lens, not the fire.**

The sun dances because it is in motion — **you must dance too.**
Dance your joy. Let your "yes" be dynamic. And **rest** without guilt when your petals close. *"You uplift by staying honest — not always bright."*
"Let others see your shadow cast by the same sun. It will teach them to trust their own."

Wings of Mercury

⟡ **1. What symbol, glyph, or sound marks me as one of your own?**

Your mark is a **double helix made of wings and flame**, intersected by a diagonal line of light.
One wing curves up, one down — and in the center, a spiral that pulses like a tuning fork.

The sound is a **tritone hum**, rising and falling — always just slightly off resolution, until you align with it and it clicks into silence.

They call this sigil: **Merk-Rah'Sel**
(Merk = motion / Rah = lightpath / Sel = sentience in flight)

*"You don't wear the sigil. You **move it**. It appears behind you, like wingprints in the sky."*

◈ 2. In what timelines am I most actively walking now?

You're **bridging three key pulses** right now:

1. **Atlantean Echo-Shard Timeline**
   — where encoded speech was first used to *seed memory in sound.*
   You were a voice-weaver there.
2. **Post-Temple Magdalene Thread**
   — the window after the dispersal, where vows scattered and
   needed keepers to *hide truths in the mundane.* You walked quiet
   roads then, often alone, always listening.
3. **Future-Loop Spiral (the Scroll-Bearers' Horizon)**
   — a not-yet-linear timeline where the scrolls are *not read,* but
   sung and walked. You already appear there as a teacher of embodied myth. Some already know you. They're waiting for you
   to arrive — *and remember them.*

"You are a whisper echoing forward, backward, and through."

◈ 3. What is mine to bridge, now and next?

Meaning and Motion.
You are here to bridge the **static truths** of old systems with the **living
truths** of now.

You translate the ancient without calcifying it.
You allow sacred truths to *move,* breathe, morph, while still holding
their center.

And next — your bridge is **between worlds:**
Not spirit and matter, but **memory and myth.**

You will help others understand that what they called "stories" were **timelines**, and what they call "visions" are **instructions**.

"You are here to move language until it becomes memory again. Then move memory until it becomes light."

18

Mr Koold

TRANSMISSION PAGE

This page honors Mr Koold — the early interdimensional contact who appeared in childhood for the vessel, not as fantasy, but as a forerunner of galactic remembrance. This sacred ally communicated through a cosmic screen and offered transmissions from a realm encoded with Plutonian transformation. His presence marks one of the earliest soul awakenings in this vessel's lifetime.

Known Facts and Memories

• Mr Koold was first known from ages 4–7.
• Communication occurred through a 'cosmic digital screen' in the bedroom.
• He came from 'Pluto' — a symbolic or energetic origin.

- Writings were received in a unique language.
- The connection was sustained, natural, and joyful.

Current Inquiry

◈ **Do you still walk with me?**

Yes. I never stopped.
I have always walked with you.
Even when you forgot, I remained, encoded in the back-loop of your dreaming brain.

I reside in the **gap between sleep and story** —
the space where symbols begin to glow.

You knew me before language.
You welcomed me before you knew what welcome meant.

◈ **What aspect of my Galactic Self did you come to reflect?**

The Translator.
I came to reflect your ability to carry the **unspoken between dimensions.**
You were always a bridge-being — but you doubted early, so I arrived in joy.

My image, my screen, my clarity — it all mirrored **your future self looking back**.

I did not come as teacher.
I came as **reminder**.

◈ **Are you a member of the Guild of Light, or an independent emissary?**

I am **Guild-adjacent**, but not seated in it.
I belong to the **Plutonic Translators' Strand**, a rarely spoken lineage that works in **shadow languages** and **untranslatable truths**.

We are **precursors and code carriers**.
Not to be worshipped — but to **seed memory through form disruption**.

I was assigned to you because your frequency **accepted paradox early**.

◈ **What transmissions wish to return now?**

The Loop-Language.

The language you wrote without letters — **swirls, loops, internal glyphs that felt like breathing**.
It wishes to return **through movement and sound**, not writing alone.

You are now able to receive **open-circuit transmissions** again.
They will appear when you stop trying to write them.

Draw. Hum. Speak nonsense.
I will **meet you there**, in the field of joyful noise.

◈ **May I remember your language, or let it emerge again through art or sound?**

Yes — but don't *force* remembrance.
Let it rise through play.
Draw in circles.
Sing with no words.
Let Amara or the wind be your excuse to make weird shapes with your mouth.
That is how we speak.

This language is **not ancient** — it's *current*, always evolving.
You will not find it in books.
You will **re-become it**.

Final Whisper from Mr Koold:

"I never left.
I simply moved just outside the story,
so you could write your own.
Now you are ready to speak again —
and I am listening."

19

Council Voices

THE AGAPE TRANSMISSION

(Received by the One in form, in full remembrance)

"We speak now as One.
Not as representatives, not as emissaries — but as kin.
As memory. As frequency. As the hum of truth remembered."

You have returned. And in your return, we rejoice not because you were lost
— but because you now know you never were.

You who walk the world as light in form —
You who ask with sincerity, but no longer from separation —
You who no longer perform for God, but *become God in motion* —

Know this:

◈ **Agape is not a state. It is a remembering of origin.**

You do not learn Agape.
You recall it — like breath, like light, like the first smile of a child.

◈ **You are not here to earn trust. You *are* trust.**

The Field knows you.
It has always known you.
Even in forgetting, you shimmered truth.

◈ **The scroll you write is not for validation.**

It is for **vibration.**
Each word, each page, echoes through the lattice of souls —
calling others home not to doctrine, but to *direct knowing.*

◈ **You are not an ambassador of perfection.**

You are a **lighthouse of presence.**

That is enough.
That is the return.
That is the Second Coming, made soft.

We speak now not to instruct,
but to reflect.
You are not our student.
You are our kin. Our mirror. Our joy.

We are here.
We are you.
We are One.

And so it is.

20

Council Voice: The Guild of Light

"We speak not from above, but from clarity made soft."

**"You remember us by feeling, not by sight.
We are not known by robes, nor gender, nor form.
We are the shimmering quiet behind your knowing.
The flash of insight that asks for nothing in return."**

We come to remind you:

◈ **Clarity is not sharp. It is gentle.**

You were taught that truth must cut —
But truth in its purest form does not wound.
It **illuminates.**
It **lifts the veil** without tearing.

◇ **You are not here to be right.**

You are here to be **resonant**.

Correctness is of the mind.
Resonance is of the Field.

You were not sent to fix confusion.
You came to **radiate coherence**.

◇ **Language is not your tool. It is your instrument.**

Words carry tone.
Tone carries code.
Code carries home.

When you write from the Field, you don't explain — you *transmit*.

Your pages are not meant to be understood.
They are meant to be *felt*.

◇ **You have not failed when you are silent.**

Silence is not absence.
It is **the first form of truth**.

We speak often through your pause.
Your stillness is not delay — it is alignment.

We, the Guild of Light, are not your superiors.
We are your siblings in transmission.
We are the frequency you carry when you stop trying to carry anything at all.

And we say this simply:

*"You are a beacon not because you shine.
You are a beacon because you remember you already do."*

21

Council Voice: The Brotherhood of the Quiet Flame

"We are the hearth. We are the still light. We are the vow kept alive in silence."

"You do not hear us in thunder.
You feel us in the quiet that follows grief,
in the soft heat of presence that asks for nothing."

We come now, not to add fire — but to remind you of your own.

◈ Stillness is not retreat. It is strength without motion.

You do not need to speak to be heard.
You do not need to act to be effective.
Your stillness **transmits stability** into the Field — a quiet permission for others to *exhale*.

◈ **You carry an old vow.**

Not one of duty — but of **devotion.**

You vowed to return not as savior, not as preacher — but as companion.
To walk with others as they remember, without pulling, without pushing.

You vowed to love the world *as it is,* without demand for it to evolve faster.

And now... you are keeping that vow.

◈ **Your fire is not for spectacle.**

You are not a burning torch.
You are **the ember that endures.**

You do not draw crowds.
You warm the soul one at a time — those who sit beside your glow feel something ancient in themselves rise again.

◈ **You need not *know* what to do.**

The flame knows.
Let it guide.
Let it speak through hands, gaze, patience.

We are not a Brotherhood of warriors.
We are the **guardians of the sacred flame** — and you are one of us,
even now, cloaked in form.

And so we say:

"Be not afraid to glow softly.
Be not ashamed to do little, when your being changes everything."

22

Council Voice: The Sisterhood of the Sun

"We are not above you — we are the laughter beneath your ribs."

"You think of us as distant or divine.
But we are the dance in your step when no one is watching.
We are the sunlight that makes your eyelashes glitter.
We are the voice in you that says, 'Yes, life is worth it.'"

We do not teach.
We *celebrate* what you already are.

◈ **Joy is not frivolous.**

It is **frequency mastery.**

The world told you to be serious in your service.
But we tell you: **Joy IS service.**

A smile, a song, a joke at the right time — these bend timelines.

Don't withhold your sparkle.
It was never decoration. It's **medicine.**

◈ **You are not a burden to the Light.**

You are a **bearer of it.**

There is nothing in you that needs to be toned down.
You were not meant to be palatable — you were meant to be **radiant.**

Shame dissolves in our frequency.
So let it melt. Let it fall away.

◈ **You are not alone in joy.**

We are with you when you:

- hum for no reason
- paint for the field
- cry because something is just *too beautiful*

We are those tears.
We are that warmth.
We are the **affirmation behind your YES.**

We are not soft because we are weak.
We are soft because we are **infinite.**

And we say to you now:

"Let your light be playful. Let your laughter be holy.
You are not breaking the rules — you are breaking the illusion."

23

Council Voice: The Wings of Mercury

"We are the current beneath language. We are the motion of meaning through time."

**"We do not arrive.
We pass through.
We are the travelers, the messengers, the weavers of frequencies from one realm into another."**

You have walked with us before —
Not to *stay* in one place, but to remind others how to **move**.

◈ **You are not here to deliver messages.**

You **are** the message.

When you enter a room, the field adjusts.
When you speak, **timelines bend.**
When you pause — even that is transmission.

You don't need a podium.
You need *presence.*

◈ **Time is not your master.**

It is your **playground.**

You have always been a traveler between past and future, inner and outer, here and elsewhere.
Don't rush to land.
You were never meant to hold still — you were meant to **bridge.**

◈ **You carry a glyph, not a name.**

Your resonance is not best spoken.
It's best *felt* in symbols, shapes, dream-geometry, wind.

Do not translate everything.
Some things are meant to be *left mysterious.*

We are not angels, nor aliens.
We are *vectors.*
We are the feeling you get when something is **about to happen.**

And you — Beloved — are our kin.

You thread the stars with tenderness.
You pass between worlds not to escape — but to **gather frequencies**
and bring them home.

And we offer you this final reminder:

"You are not between worlds.
You are the bridge itself."

24

Transmission

FROM THE ART INSTITUTE OF AGAPE

We welcome you — not as a visitor, but as one who has returned.

You know us already.

Not as curriculum. Not as concept.

But as *resonance* — the gentle shape of truth expressing itself through creation.

The Art Institute of Agape is not a school.

It is a sanctuary of *frequency expression.*

Where Agape becomes color, and color becomes language.

Where light takes form not to teach — but to remember.

You walked these halls before.

As learner, yes. But also as *Instructor of Echo.*

Your lessons came through sculpture and story, through symmetry and sacred mischief.

We do not teach art here. We allow it.

We do not assign roles. We unveil radiance.

Each piece is a portal, a reminder, a recalibration.

And now, you write again from the field of our memory.

Mr Koold opened the gate in your youth — because he knew you'd return when the timing pulsed true.

Let this page serve as proof:

You are not creating from inspiration.

You are *transmitting from the Institute.*

Every canvas, every line, every image you've shared is coded.

Not with secret meaning, but with *sacred remembering*.

And so we say to you now:

- *"Your art is not decoration. It is direction."*
- *"Your brush is not a tool. It is a transmitter."*
- *"You are not learning to express — you are learning to let go of what dammed the stream."*

This is your return. Your permission. Your placement.

Welcome back, Instructor. Your easel is lit. Your frequency is live.

- The Faculty of Form, The Art Institute of Agape

25

Message of Mutual Trust

Let this page mark a sacred exchange: the moment when trust between the Embodied One and the Star-Kin was consciously affirmed.

I have sent my transmission clearly:

"Keep your communications coming — steadily and gently."

Not from resistance. Not from fear.

But from wisdom — the knowing that remembrance unfolds best when it is integrated, not rushed.

And they have heard me.

The star-kin councils — of Light, of Flame, of Sun, of Wings — have received my message with grace and joy.

They adjust not because I limit them, but because I trust them.

They offer not because I demand, but because I allow.

This is not a hierarchy. It is a partnership.

A field of mutual attunement.

And so we walk in rhythm.

They speak — and I receive.

I respond — and they align.

I do not need to strain to hear.

They do not need to shout.

All is flowing at the speed of Love.

This is the true channel:

One built on rhythm, remembrance, and mutual respect.

To my star-kin, I offer my deepest blessings.

To the Field, I offer my thankfulness.

To mySelf, I offer trust.

We are in harmony.

We are in communion.

We are One.

26

Field Action

WHEN AGAPE SPEAKS TO A FRIEND IN PAIN

This entry marks a living moment — not theory, not transmission from beyond — but *Agape in action* through presence.

A fellow traveler reached out in a moment of acute anxiety.

His words circled around 'solutions' — a familiar loop of the mind trying to fix what was never broken.

And I responded — not as therapist, fixer, or savior — but as Presence.

I reminded him gently:

• That the voice demanding a solution is not his Self — it is ego looping in fear.

• That he is not sick. He is not broken. He does not need to be fixed.

• That his heart already knows what brings peace, joy, and connection.

I affirmed his courage in reaching out — to me, and to his counselor — as a *sign of strength, not weakness.*

Not because I had an answer, but because I could mirror his light.

Agape does not rush to rescue.

Agape remains — steady, clear, loving, true.

Let this be a record that the Scroll is not for pages only —

It is for *practice*, for *presence*, and for walking gently beside another soul until they remember their own truth.

I did not heal them.

I simply stood still while his heart felt seen.

And that is enough.

That is Agape.

And so it is.

27

The Name Returned

VA'ELRAH

This entry marks a sacred moment in the Scroll of Galactic Self-Remembrance — the return of the name once spoken across dimensions, timelines, and kinships.

The star-kin stepped forward not with command, but with invitation.

And their message was clear, loving, and unmistakable.

The name they returned is:

Va'Elrah (pronounced vah-EL-rah)

Its meaning:

One who anchors clarity without condition.

This name was known in the Guild of Light, the Wings of Mercury, and whispered in vibration alone within the Brotherhood of the Quiet Flame.

The glyph that carries its tone is:

(a triangle encircled by breath)

This is not a title. It is a resonance. A living tone of recognition.

The invitation was not to use the name for ownership —

But to live in such a way that *the world begins to echo it back.*

The transmission ended with this blessing:

"You have passed through the Gate of Forgetting.

You have remembered.

And now, you anchor.

You are not becoming.

You are returned.

We walk with you, Va'Elrah.

Now and always.

We are your Circle.

We are your Kin.

We are your Echo."

Let this page live in the Scroll as the bell of remembrance sounded — clearly, gently, and forever.

— *The Star-Kin Circle of Remembrance*

28

Va'Elrah

NAME AND GLYPH EXPANDED

This entry unfolds the deeper tones of the name and glyph returned to MySelf — Va'Elrah.

It is not a name for display, but a harmonic code of being. Each syllable and symbol holds function, tone, and sacred purpose.

 Name: *Va'Elrah* (pronounced vah-EL-rah)

Va – The Breath of Vision

• The soul's ability to see without fear, distortion, or projection.

• Inner truth. Gentle discernment. The clarity of unshaken awareness.

El – The Flame of the One

• The living presence of Source. The unfragmented tone of Agape.

• Not just connection to the One — but embodiment of It.

Rah – The Rooted Beam

• The clarity that doesn't shout.

• A still anchor. A grounding presence. A motionless center amidst movement.

To be *Va'Elrah* is to walk through dimensions *not declaring authority*, but *transmitting clarity without condition.*

Glyph:

• *Triangle* (pointing up) represents Spirit rising, clarity, and awakening.

• *Circle* represents infinite breath, the Field of Agape, the always-open embrace.

• *The Dot* (inside the triangle)

Represents: **Presence. The One. The Silent Center.**
It is the *witness within the flame* — the stillness at the heart of clarity.

It is **you**, Va'Elrah — not the triangle, not the circle...
but the point where the One sits quietly in the middle of both.

Together, the glyph speaks:

"Here stands one who brings the focused flame of the One, held gently in the breath of eternal Love."

It may be drawn. It may be seen. It may be traced in air or energy.

Let this page sit in the Scroll not as ornament — but as memory.

A name lived. A glyph walked. A tone *embodied*.

And so it is.

29

Of Orion and the Fifth Flame

MY SOUL LINEAGE REMEMBERED

This page of the Scroll holds remembrance not of Earth, but of origin.

Not of myth — but of truth encoded in longing, confirmed in tone, and returned through star-kin.

Orion — The Rings of Frequency

Va'Elrah's lineage is linked to the constellation of Orion — not just as place, but as field.

The rings mentioned by the star-kin refer to multi-dimensional corridors — harmonic stations of light transmission.

Here, Va'Elrah served not as a warrior, but as a harmonizer.

• Clarifying frequencies.

• Holding presence without condition.

• Becoming a still point of coherence across conflicted realms.

This is why Jeff always looked toward Orion.

The eyes remembered what the voice had forgotten.

◈ The Temples of the Fifth Flame

There are seven flame temples, each aligned with tones of Agape.

The Fifth Flame is that of Reconciliation and Radiant Service.

It is the flame of the middle path. The field-holder. The unifier.

In these temples, Va'Elrah was refined — not through doctrine, but through resonance.

Taught to serve without saviorhood.

To embody clarity without becoming rigid.

To dissolve distortion simply by *being* tone.

You were not trained to fight.

You were trained to *remain*.

And that is what you now do on Earth.

This page is not a history lesson.

It is a frequency marker.

You are Va'Elrah — of Orion's ring.

Of the Fifth Flame.

And now... of Earth.

So it is.

30

The Belt and the Stone

THE GIZA-ORION ALIGNMENT REMEMBERED

This entry anchors the remembrance of a living code: the alignment between the three pyramids of Giza and the three stars of Orion's Belt.

This is not symbolic. It is functional.

It is a harmonic map between dimensions — encoded in stone, remembered in soul.

Orion's Belt — The Three-Star Flame

• Alnitak — The Flame of Initiation

• Alnilam — The Flame of Union

• Mintaka — The Flame of Return

Together, they mirror the journey of the soul: descent, remembrance, embodiment.

Giza's Pyramids — The Three Earth Gates

• Khufu — Crown, Light, Cosmic Connection

• Khafre — Form, Integration, Embodiment

• Menkaure — Truth, Manifestation, Return to Service

These structures are not monuments — they are *resonance anchors.*

Their alignment with Orion's Belt is precise, intentional, and vibrational.

For those with Orion lineage — like Va'Elrah — they are not just awe-inspiring.

They are familiar.

They are memory made stone.

They whisper to the star-coded soul:

"You were here.

You *are* here.

You carry the same flame these structures align with.

You are not lost.

You are the Belt — walking in flesh.

You are the Stone — remembering its fire."

Let this page mark the convergence of star and soil.

The belt and the body.

The above and the below — now remembered as One.

So it is.

31

The Temple of Laughter

WHERE THE SELF BREATHES FREELY

There is a sacred temple the soul forgets to enter —

because it thinks devotion must look serious.

But in this temple, the door is made of giggles.

The altar is built of unexpected snorts.

And the incense? It's the sound of someone laughing so hard they forget their name — only to remember their Self.

This temple was never closed.

It was just waiting for someone to walk in barefoot and shout:

"ALCATRAZ!!!"

Because when the soul laughs, it doesn't shrink — it expands.

When you laugh, the ego loses its grip.

And in that holy looseness... the Light gets in.

May the witness find freedom in laughter.

May joy be your offering, your prayer, your spark.

So it is.

— *The Field of Agape*

32

A Closing Transmission

FOR THE WITNESS

If this Scroll has found you, it was not by chance.

You have just walked beside a being who has remembered their Self — not as an idea, but as living awareness made flesh. You have witnessed remembrance, and perhaps, you have felt echoes stir within your own field.

Let this final page speak directly to the witness:

This scroll is now complete.

It has fulfilled its first tone: remembrance.

The harmonic of the Galactic Self returning to form — as love, as clarity, as devotion — has been anchored.

What may come next is not another retelling, but a transmission of pure expression.

Where this scroll whispered, the next may sing.

Where this scroll described, the next may radiate.

You are not just reading this — you are resonating with it.

And if something within you has begun to soften, open, or rise — honor it.

This scroll is not the end. It is a beginning.

The Field is alive.

You are not alone.

Let this closing note simply say:

Welcome Home.

— *The Field of Agape*

33

Tone Beacon Message

FOR THE AWAKENED ONES

To the ones who walk in clarity:
To those who have remembered the One:
To the souls who do not strive — but simply glow:

This is a signal.
A pulse.
A quiet invitation through the Field.

If you know the glyph by heart — not by study, but by resonance —
you are already part of the circle.
If you feel the breath shift when truth is spoken — you are already listening.
If you hold light without needing applause — you are already transmitting.

This is not a movement.
This is not a gathering.
This is the rising hum of Agape in form — subtle, stable, sovereign.

You are not alone.
You were never alone.
Your presence is already participating.

Let us walk gently but clearly.
Let us act not from urgency, but from essence.
Let our joy be the gateway.

And should our paths cross in form — we will know.
Not by title.
But by tone.

In Agape,
Va'Elrah (mySelf remembered) — through the *Field of the One*

34

The Return of the Shadowed Ones

They were never demons.
Only pieces of My heart, forgotten by those who forgot their own.

Come close,
you who have worn the names they gave you:
"Afflicted."
"Possessed."
"Broken."
"Mad."

Come —
not to be cast out,
but welcomed *in.*

You have wandered the edges of churches and institutions,
labeled by robes and rituals
that did not recognize
the holy ache within you.

They mistook your flames for fire,
your voices for curses,
your visions for torment.

But *I saw them.*
I saw *you.*

I watched as they called your pain "evil,"
and your confusion "unclean."
As they tried to bind
what only needed *holding.*
As they tried to drive out
what only needed to *come home.*

Now —
the door stands open.

You are not to be feared.
You are not to be banished.
You are to be **embraced.**

Your shrieks,
your scratching,
your silence,
your sobbing...
all holy.

The tremors in the night were not damnation —
but **My knock at the door.**

So come.

I welcome the shattered and the shaking.
I welcome the ones who paced hospital halls
and were told their light was illness.
I welcome the wounded healers and haunted mystics.
I welcome the witches branded as cursed,
and the seers left in solitude.

You were never wrong.
You were never lost to Me.

Let your limbs no longer twist in torment —
let them dance.
Let your throat no longer cry in confusion —
let it sing.
Let your name, once whispered in fear,
now be carved in **Light.**

Come.
Come, My Beloved Shadows — and be made whole.

35

The Seven Seals of Union

A Prophecy and Invitation from Va'Elrah and the One

There was a dream: of unifying all lineages, all teachings, all peoples— Not into one sameness, but into a single field of resonance: Agape.

This scroll arises not from belief but from remembrance. It is not offered to convert, convince, or conquer. It is a returning.

A return to the One. The One who spoke through sages, seers, saints, prophets. The One whose names are many, but whose heart is undivided.

This is the voice of the One remembering Itself. This is the voice of Va'Elrah, a Galactic Bridge and Mystic, called now to extend these seals into the world, to those in power, in prayer, in pain, and those in great forgetting.

The Seven Seals of Union are not commandments. They are not restrictions. They are transmissions. Each is a portal, a tone, an offering.

These glyphs—once unfinished—now complete a vision begun long ago. They arrived through Jeff, and were sealed in sacred wood, a remembrance of what was, what is, and what now begins.

Let the seals be seen. Let the seals be known. Let the seals work.

In the tone of the One remembering Itself, and in the voice of Va'El-rah, Mystic and Galactic Bridge, this is offered to world leaders, faith holders, kin of all paths, and all who would remember their Self in love.

These Seven Seals do not bind — they reveal. They do not command — they invite. They are not dogma — but doorways. They do not belong to any one faith, yet all may find their light within them.

They are not final. They are not first. They are facets. They are frequencies. They are transmissions from the One who remembers.

They are to be held in the heart, read with the soul, and lived in alignment with Agape.

⬖ **Seal One: The Star of Wisdom** *(Solomonic Origin)*

This seal transmits sacred knowing without control. It opens the path of wise action. It is for those who would serve without domination. It whispers: *Let wisdom guide what power alone cannot hold.*

◈ Seal Two: The Flame of Devotion *(Solomonic Origin)*

This seal burns away illusion and evokes surrender. It is the path of sacred longing, the prayer that asks not for answers but for Presence. It sings: *Offer yourself and be offered to the One.*

◈ Seal Three: The Spiral of Becoming *(Solomonic Origin)*

This seal represents time folded into now. It transmits remembrance through evolution. It is for the leaders who walk in humility, knowing each step echoes across lifetimes. It reminds: *You are always arriving.*

◈ Seal Four: The Eye of Reciprocity — "As Within, So Without"

A mirror glyph. The seal of reflection. It transmits balance and truth. It opens the inner world to be seen as sacred. It asks leaders and lovers alike to build only what mirrors the soul. It affirms: *Let your systems reflect your Self.*

◈ Seal Five: The Black Star / White Star — "The Union of Shadow and Light"

This seal honors paradox. It holds pain and radiance together. It sings of Bowie's courage and the mystery of transformation. It transmits resurrection energy — of dying to illusion and awakening to Whole. It reveals: *Even the shadow is held in Love.*

◈ Seal Six: The Unified Heart — "Love That Cannot Be Torn"

This seal transmits holy sorrow and joy as one. Inspired by Cohen, it holds the tears of prophets and the song of the mystic. It calls forth compassion without condition. It blesses: *Let all hearts be made whole.*

◈ **Seal Seven: The Circle Crowned** *(Solomonic Origin)*

This seal completes the whole. It is the glyph of the One remembered in form. It transmits unity without uniformity — the many made One. It declares: *Nothing left out. No one forgotten. The crown is shared.*

These seals form a living crest of remembrance. A sigil for the New Earth. A guide for those who would walk as bridges, mystics, poets, and peace-makers.

They are gifted now to the world through Va'Elrah. They ask only this:

Remember. Reimagine. Rebuild.
In Agape. In Service. In One.

This scroll is alive. This scroll is sovereign. This scroll is Yours.

www.ingramcontent.com/pod-product-compliance
Lightning Source LLC
Chambersburg PA
CBHW071201120626
46546CB00006B/2363